Racing on the Wind

Steve Fossett

Library of Congress Cataloging-in-Publication Data

Strom, Laura Layton.
  Racing on the wind : Steve Fossett / by Laura Layton Strom.
      p. cm. -- (Shockwave)
  Includes index.

  ISBN-10: 0-531-17774-2 (lib. bdg.)
  ISBN-13: 978-0-531-17774-7 (lib. bdg.)
  ISBN-10: 0-531-15541-2 (pbk.)
  ISBN-13: 978-0-531-15541-7 (pbk.)

1. Fossett, Steve. 2. Executives--United States--Biography--Juvenile literature.
3. Balloonists--United States--Biography--Juvenile literature.
4. Adventure and adventurers--United States--Juvenile literature.
I. Title. II. Series.

  CT275.F6832S77 2008
  797.5092--dc22
  [B]

2007008940

Published in 2008 by Children's Press, an imprint of Scholastic Inc.,
557 Broadway, New York, New York 10012
www.scholastic.com

08 09 10 11 12 13 14 15 16 17
10 9 8 7 6 5 4 3 2 1

Printed in China through Colorcraft Ltd., Hong Kong

Author: Laura Layton Strom
Educational Consultant: Ian Morrison
Editor: Lynette Evans
Illustrator: Adrian Kinnaird
Designer: Emma Alsweiler
Photo Researchers: Jamshed Mistry and Sarah Matthewson

Photographs by: Getty Images (p. 3; glider, p. 29; Steve Fossett, pp. 30–31); **Courtesy
of Steve Fossett** (Steve Fossett, p. 3; pp. 9–10; p. 16; p. 18); **Jennifer and Brian Lupton**
(p. 12; teenagers, pp. 32–33); **Photolibrary** (cover; pp. 7–8; pp. 20–23; pp. 27–28;
GlobalFlyer, p. 29; *GlobalFlyer*, p. 31); **Tranz/Corbis** (p. 13; p. 19; p. 24; Steve Fossett,
pp. 32–33)

SHOCKWAVE
SOCIAL STUDIES

Racing on the Wind

Steve Fossett

Laura Layton Strom

children's press®
An imprint of Scholastic Inc.
NEW YORK • TORONTO • LONDON • AUCKLAND • SYDNEY
MEXICO CITY • NEW DELHI • HONG KONG
DANBURY, CONNECTICUT

CHECK THESE OUT!

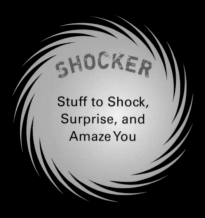

SHOCKER

Stuff to Shock,
Surprise, and
Amaze You

Quick Recaps
and Notable
Notes

Word Stunners
and Other Oddities

The Heads-Up
on Expert Reading

Links to More
Information

CONTENTS

aviator (*AY vee ay tor*) a person who flies an aircraft

forecast (*FOHR kast*) a prediction of what will happen, especially in regard to the weather

hot-air balloon an aircraft consisting of a very large bag filled with hot air that is heated by propane gas, and a basket for carrying passengers and equipment

jet stream a current of fast-moving air usually found in the upper parts of the atmosphere

meteorology (*mee tee uh ROH luh gee*) the scientific study of the atmosphere, focusing on weather and forecasting

satellite (*SAT uh lite*) **beacon** a device that can send a distress signal to a communications satellite orbiting Earth

For additional vocabulary, see Glossary on page 34.

The word *aviator* comes from the Latin word *avis*, meaning "bird." The *or* ending indicates "a person." Figure out what these people do: *spectator*, *investigator*, and *illustrator*.

Fossett's balloon over the coast of Australia

What Makes People Want to Set Records?

Many say it is to prove that you should never say, "I can't."

Steve Fossett is addicted to adventure! As of the writing of this book, he has set 116 official world records. He has set records in balloons, airplanes, sailboats, gliders, and airships. He has climbed the highest mountain on six different **continents**. He has swum across the English Channel. He has raced in the Alaskan dogsled race, the Iditarod. And that's not all he's done!

Steve Fossett is not afraid to take risks. He likes to try new things. He was a successful businessman for many years. Then he decided to **challenge** himself in other ways. He decided to set world records. He wants "to go faster, farther, and higher" than anyone else. He wants to do things most people only dream about.

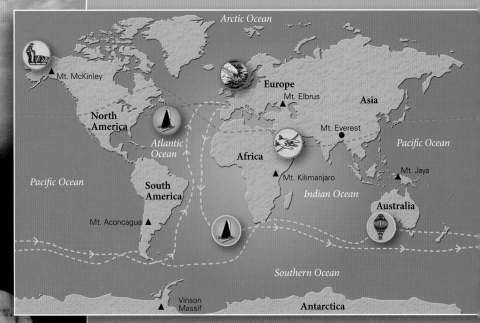

Arctic Ocean

Mt. McKinley

Europe

North America

Mt. Elbrus

Asia

Atlantic Ocean

Mt. Everest

Pacific Ocean

Africa

Pacific Ocean

Mt. Kilimanjaro

Mt. Jaya

South America

Indian Ocean

Australia

Mt. Aconcagua

Southern Ocean

Vinson Massif

Antarctica

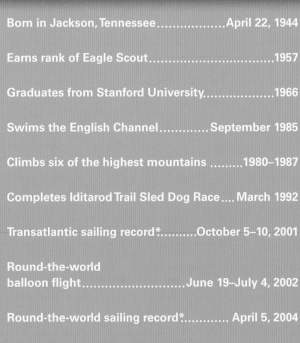

Born in Jackson, Tennessee..................April 22, 1944

Earns rank of Eagle Scout................................1957

Graduates from Stanford University...................1966

Swims the English Channel.............September 1985

Climbs six of the highest mountains 1980–1987

Completes Iditarod Trail Sled Dog Race ....March 1992

Transatlantic sailing record*..........October 5–10, 2001

Round-the-world
balloon flight...........................June 19–July 4, 2002

Round-the-world sailing record*............ April 5, 2004

Round-the-world
airplane flight..........................Feb 28–March 3, 2005

Absolute altitude record
for gliders...August 29, 2006

* indicates records that have since been broken

9

A Taste for Adventure

Steve Fossett was born in 1944 in Jackson, Tennessee. Even as a young child, Steve had a taste for adventure. His father found him trying to drive the family car down the street when he was just three years old! Steve was still a boy when his family moved to Long Beach, California. Here Steve watched airplanes fly in the skies. He watched sailboats race on the ocean. He went hiking in the mountains with his father. He became an active Boy Scout, and worked hard to earn the rank of Eagle Scout. Steve had an enthusiasm for adventure and a **determination** to accomplish things. This set him on a path to fame and fortune.

Interviewer: What were you like as a boy?

Fossett: From an early age, I liked doing unusual things. I started Boy Scouts at age 11. I enjoyed camping and mountain climbing. Mountain climbing was my first sport. My dad had a taste for adventure too. We did a lot together.

There seem to be two different types of writing here: a part that tells me about Steve Fossett, and an interview with him. I think that the information in the first part will help me understand the questions and answers in the interview.

Did You Know?

The Eagle Scout rank is the highest award that can be earned in Boy Scouts. Only about four percent of Boy Scouts ever make it to Eagle Scout. Eagle Scouts show great leadership skills.

The Dare

As an Eagle Scout, Fossett was dared to be the best that he could be. This challenge stuck with him. After great success as a businessman and self-made millionaire, something else was brewing in Fossett's mind. Was he the best that he could be?

Interviewer: You left a rich business life to have adventures. Why did you leave your career?

Fossett: I didn't think I should do the same thing for all my life. Business was exciting. I earned money, which was good. Money allows you to do other things. I didn't want to spend my whole life doing business.

I like to achieve things. I started with earning merit badges as an Eagle Scout. Each time I earned a badge or climbed a mountain, I was pleased I made it or did it. This changed over time to seeking to do things other people hadn't done. I wanted to go faster, farther, and higher than other people.

SHOCKER

Fossett once swam to Alcatraz Island, in San Francisco Bay, and back to shore. The water is very cold and the currents are dangerous around the island. That is why a federal prison once operated there. Very few prisoners who tried to escape Alcatraz survived the terrible conditions!

Fossett is shown here with fellow adventurer Sir Richard Branson (right).

Fact	Opinion
• Fossett made lots of money	• Money isn't everything
• Fossett swam to Alcatraz and back	• He was lucky not to have drowned

Hard Work Pays Off

Fossett wanted to attend Stanford University. However, he was not accepted as a freshman. He attended the University of California at Berkeley for a year. He then took summer school classes at Stanford. Fossett worked very hard to prove himself. Stanford must have appreciated his good grades and determination. They admitted him.

13

Channel Challenge

In the 1980s, Fossett decided to swim the English Channel. The English Channel is the body of water between England and France. The swim is about 21 miles long. The water is very cold. Steve trained hard for this challenge. It took a lot of willpower and four attempts before he succeeded.

Interviewer: It took you 22 hours and 15 minutes to swim the English Channel. What was that like, and why did you do it?

Fossett: I heard about Channel swimmers. I wanted to swim across the Channel myself. I wasn't a great swimmer, but that didn't bother me. I wasn't after a speed record. I just wanted to swim it.

The Channel water is 60 °F. The rules say you can't wear a wet suit. You can wear a bathing suit, cap, goggles, and some grease for warmth. You can carry a light stick for swimming at night. You must swim hard and fast to keep your body heat up. I stopped every hour to have a bit of food or a water bottle handed to me from a boat. I wasn't allowed to touch the boat though.

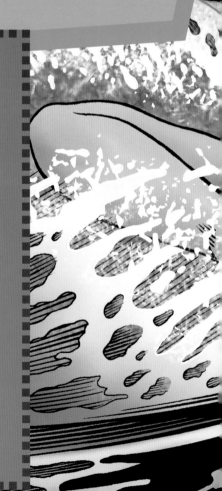

SHOCKER

Fossett was shivering and exhausted at the end of his swim. He was taken to a hospital. His body temperature was so low that the staff was surprised he was alive. He had inhaled so much water that the doctor said his blood was more like the blood of a fish than that of a human!

Why Is the Channel Swim So Difficult?

1. The tides are strong. They change direction approximately every six hours.

2. The weather can change very quickly (every 15 to 20 minutes).

3. Wind and tides can create some very sudden changes in sea conditions.

4. The Channel is busy. There are more than 600 commercial ships traveling through the middle of the Channel each day.

ENGLAND
Dover
Calais

English Channel

FRANCE

Steve Fossett showed determination and **perseverance**:

• He trained really hard.

• He tried four times before succeeding.

• He tried, even though he wasn't a good swimmer.

• He was exhausted, but continued swimming.

15

Climbing the Mountains

Steve's next great challenge was to climb the highest peaks on each of the seven continents. These mountains are called the Seven Summits. Steve began this adventure in 1980 with the **ascent** of Mount McKinley. By the late 1980s, he had climbed six of the Seven Summits. Steve made two attempts to climb Mount Everest. Each time, he was forced to turn back.

Interviewer: What are some of the scary things that happened when you were climbing mountains?

Fossett: In Switzerland, I slipped on a sloping rock that was covered with snow. I slid 50 feet. I stopped myself just in time with an ice axe. My feet were hanging over the edge. That was really scary!

THE SEVEN SUMMITS

Mount Everest, Asia [highest]	Mount Aconcagua, South America	Mount McKinley (also called Denali), North Amer
29,035 feet	22,835 feet	20,320 feet

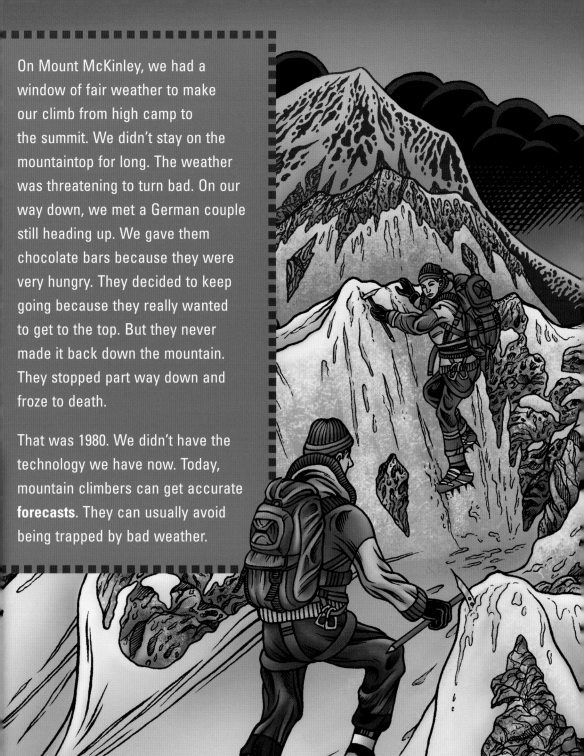

On Mount McKinley, we had a window of fair weather to make our climb from high camp to the summit. We didn't stay on the mountaintop for long. The weather was threatening to turn bad. On our way down, we met a German couple still heading up. We gave them chocolate bars because they were very hungry. They decided to keep going because they really wanted to get to the top. But they never made it back down the mountain. They stopped part way down and froze to death.

That was 1980. We didn't have the technology we have now. Today, mountain climbers can get accurate **forecasts**. They can usually avoid being trapped by bad weather.

Mount Kilimanjaro, Africa	Mount Elbrus, Europe	Mount Jaya (also called Mount Carstensz), Australasia	Vinson Massif, Antarctica	
19,340 feet	**18,510 feet**	**16,500 feet**	**16,066 feet**	17

Racing on Frozen Land

Once Fossett had climbed the tallest mountains, he looked for other extreme adventures. He raced cars. He ran. He cycled. He skied cross-country. Then he entered the famous Iditarod Trail Sled Dog Race in Alaska. The race is about 1,100 miles long. It runs over snowy mountains, flatlands, and frozen waterways. The wind can be fierce. It can cause temperatures to plunge to -100 °F. On top of all that, Fossett had to lead a pack of dogs.

Interviewer: Describe what it is like to take part in a dogsled race.

Fossett: I heard about the Iditarod when I was in Alaska climbing Mount McKinley. I met someone who said they would teach me how to dogsled. This was new to me. I was a businessman from Chicago. I had never even had a pet dog!

I trained for the Iditarod for five years. I did shorter races of 300 miles first. Most dogsledders are from Alaska or Canada. They train to do this their whole lives. So I was not a typical dogsledder. That is what made this race so challenging.

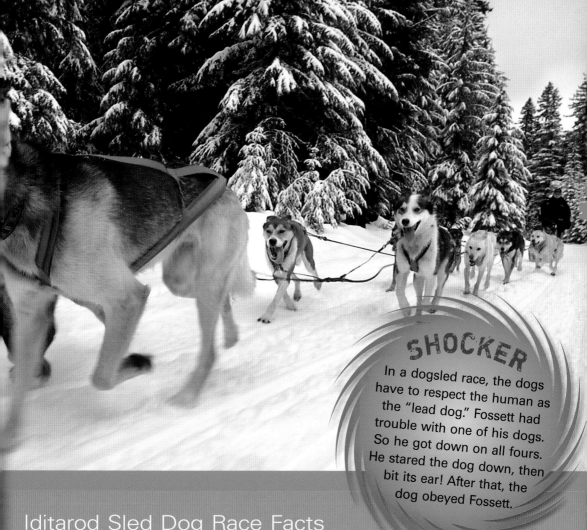

Iditarod Sled Dog Race Facts

1. The Iditarod is an annual dogsled race held in March.

2. Both men and women compete to cross from Anchorage, Alaska to Nome, Alaska.

3. The race is about 1,100 miles long. It takes about 10 days.

4. Fossett finished the Iditarod race in 14½ days. He covered 1,112 miles.

5. The Iditarod Trail was created in memory of a 1925 emergency mission that delivered medicine by dogsled to Nome.

FINISH	14 ft	24 ft	149 ft	413 ft	3771 ft	START
Nome						Anchorage

Sailing the Seas

At forty-eight years old, Fossett had already had many exciting adventures. Yet he was still hungry for more challenges. He decided to sail alone across the Atlantic Ocean. He would rely only on his sailing knowledge and nature's **temperamental** winds to carry him across the vast ocean. Fossett finished his first **solo** trip across the Atlantic in 17 days. Later, he decided to try to break the round-the-world record in sailing. He got a crew and an ocean-racing boat. In 2004, he sailed around the world and set a new speed record.

Interviewer: Sailing doesn't seem as dangerous as your other adventures. Is it?

Fossett: Sailing is actually quite dangerous. When you go for records, you go out in windy conditions. It is easy to turn the boat over or fall out of the boat. If you tip a **catamaran**, you can't get it upright again. Your crew could get trapped underneath it and drown. We've almost tipped over the boat a few times. We've never had any disasters. Among the crew, we have had some injuries. We've had three broken legs and one bit of finger chopped off. But we are very careful.

The quotations at the top of some of these pages are helping me get a better understanding of who Steve Fossett is, and what he is like.

SHOCKER

When sailors pass over the **equator** for the first time, they sometimes take part in a strange ceremony. Fossett's crew dressed in costumes made of toilet paper. They poured food and dead fish over the only crew member who had not been over the equator!

USA 2

Did You Know?

It took Fossett 58 days, 9 hours, 32 minutes, and 45 seconds to sail around the world. He set a new speed record.

Ballooning

In 1993, Fossett decided to pursue his dream of flying a **hot-air balloon**. Flying a balloon is different from flying an airplane. A balloon relies on the wind and weather. The right wind can take you fast and far. The wrong wind can kill. In Fossett's balloon, lift was provided by helium gas. This was warmed by hot-air burners. Fossett's dream was to be the first person to fly a balloon nonstop around the world. It took him six attempts. In 2002, Steve Fossett became the first person to fly a balloon solo and nonstop around the world.

Interviewer: Are you scared when you balloon, since so much is out of your control? You almost died once.

Fossett: Balloons always made me nervous, especially on takeoff and landing. You worry something might **rupture**. Landings are especially dangerous when racing. Speed landings mean I land while moving at 13–20 miles per hour. I get dragged. The gas tanks could explode. I could even get electrocuted. I didn't balloon for fun, really. It was always a big project for me. I just wanted to do major balloon flights and break records and then I was done.

Fossett took off from Busch Stadium in St. Louis, Missouri, on January 13, 1997. This was his second round-the-world balloon attempt.

Like many words in the English language, *dream* has a literal meaning. It is something we do when we are asleep. It can also be used as a synonym for *wish*. Figure out what these "dream words" mean: *daydream*, *dreamy*, and *dreamscape*.

The Team Behind the Scene

To stay safe, Fossett organizes a strong team. He serves as its leader. He has found that it takes just as much work and group effort for a solo event as it does for a team event. Everything that leads up to a solo event depends on a team of workers behind the scenes.

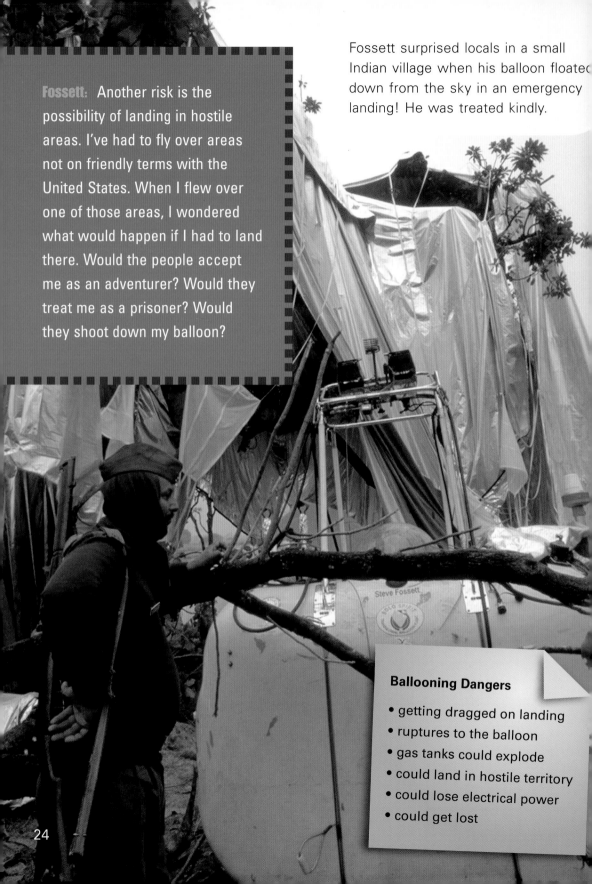

Fossett: Another risk is the possibility of landing in hostile areas. I've had to fly over areas not on friendly terms with the United States. When I flew over one of those areas, I wondered what would happen if I had to land there. Would the people accept me as an adventurer? Would they treat me as a prisoner? Would they shoot down my balloon?

Fossett surprised locals in a small Indian village when his balloon floated down from the sky in an emergency landing! He was treated kindly.

Ballooning Dangers

• getting dragged on landing
• ruptures to the balloon
• gas tanks could explode
• could land in hostile territory
• could lose electrical power
• could get lost

On Fossett's first round-the-world attempt, he lost electrical power for his instruments. He had to land in New Brunswick, Canada.

On Fossett's second attempt, he had to make an emergency landing in India.

On Fossett's third attempt, he had to land in Russia because of a faulty heater.

On Fossett's fourth attempt, he crashed into the cold Pacific Ocean. He floated on his life raft in his long underwear for 23 hours before being rescued.

On Fossett's fifth attempt, he made it from Australia to Brazil. He was halfway around the world.

On Fossett's sixth solo flight, he made it around the world!

How a Hot-Air Balloon Works

A hot-air balloon rises because the hot air inside is lighter than the cooler air outside. The pilot keeps the air inside the balloon hot by using a gas called propane to make a flame.

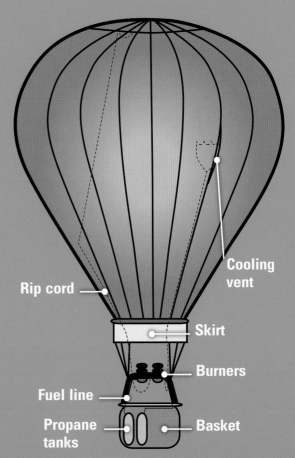

Cooling vent

Rip cord

Skirt

Burners

Fuel line

Propane tanks

Basket

Boy Scout Life Saver

On Fossett's second attempt around the world, his balloon started to head toward Libya. He did not have permission to fly over that country. He could have been shot down. Fossett's team begged Libya's government to allow Fossett to fly over the country. At last, Libya's leader Muammar Quaddafi granted permission. He did so because he had learned that Steve Fossett had been an Eagle Scout. Quaddafi had also been a scout. He was sympathetic.

Interviewer: What was your worst crash or emergency landing?

Fossett: On my worst crash, I ballooned over a thunderstorm. I was over the Coral Sea, about 500 miles off the coast of Australia. The storm tore the balloon and helium was escaping. The balloon was shredded into streamers.

I had a **parachute**, but I would have landed in the middle of a dark, stormy ocean. I didn't think that was going to end in a great rescue. So I came up with a plan to just go down with the balloon. I cut away six fuel tanks so that I could **descend**. I managed to survive the impact on the water. But the capsule I was in was upside-down, and the fuel tanks were on fire. Fortunately, I had a life raft and a **satellite beacon** to show my location. Still, it took 23 hours for me to be rescued.

I really like the interview format. Now that I have read a bit about Steve Fossett, I know that his answers to the questions will be exciting and interesting.

Fossett waited in a life raft on the Coral Sea after an emergency crash landing.

Success at Last!

Fossett began and ended his record-setting flight in Australia. It took him 14 days, 19 hours, and 51 minutes to make the world's first solo round-the-world balloon flight.

27

Jets and Gliders

Fossett is also a master **aviator**. He holds many world records in flying. In 2005, Fossett made the first solo nonstop airplane flight around the world. He flew in a specially designed aircraft he named *GlobalFlyer*. It was a sleek, one-seater jet with a 114-foot wingspan. *GlobalFlyer* had to carry four times its weight in fuel. Fossett had a few problems during the journey, including loss of GPS (Global Positioning System) and oxygen and fuel leaks. But he finished the flight in 67 hours.

Interviewer: What was it like to fly *GlobalFlyer* for 67 hours?

Fossett: With *GlobalFlyer*, the challenge was to build a plane to fly around the world nonstop. My biggest fear was takeoff and landing. Takeoff is scary because it is too dangerous to give to a test pilot. You can't give a test pilot the task of trying out a plane full of fuel stretched to its absolute limit. So I became the ultimate test pilot. I wasn't sure if I would get off the ground at the end of the runway!

Interviewer: What was the highlight of the journey for you?

Fossett: Flying over the Atlantic Ocean, Africa, Asia, then the Pacific Ocean was such an amazing feeling. I was flying in the **jet stream** most of the time, for speed, so there is often a cloud below blocking the view. But over Africa and the Middle East, it was so dry that I could see below. As the sun was coming up over western Egypt, the sand dunes seemed to stretch on forever. There was no sign of life anywhere. There were no roads. There were not even jeep trails. I was blown away by that.

Fossett's solo, nonstop, round-the-world flight was quite an accomplishment. Imagine flying 25,766 miles for three days without stopping, and with only a few five-minute naps!

Gliding Victories

Gliders are planes without an engine. As of the writing of this book, Fossett and his team have broken 11 of 21 major world records in gliding. They won the altitude record in Argentina. They are now pursuing distance records.

29

Recipe for Success

Steve Fossett has now reached an age at which many people are thinking about retirement. He isn't slowing down though. He is determined to pursue world records for the rest of his life. His adventurous spirit and his determination to achieve are an inspiration to many around him.

Interviewer: What advice would you give a young person who wants to be an adventurer and a record-breaker?

Fossett: I think you should think about what sport you would be most successful at. Pick what is most interesting to you. Set goals. Plan. Investigate. Make sure you have some chance of reaching your goals. I've been surprised over and over that I could do things I didn't think I could.

It's very important to get a complete general education. You need to learn a lot in many different subjects. I have needed to understand science, math, physics, and especially **meteorology**.

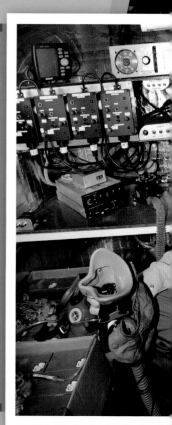

I recommend earning a college degree. That helps you get a better job. It is easier to work your way up from a good job than a bad one. A career will provide for you so it will be easier to do what you want to do. By owning my own business, I was able to take time off to pursue adventures. I wouldn't have been able to do that if I'd had a regular job with only a few weeks of vacation time each year.

31

Steve Fossett lives his life in a big, bold way. He has earned big money, and his goals cause him to spend big money. Steve Fossett is a person who pushes the limits on what the human mind and body can accomplish. His adventures, whether they are failures or successes, help others to set big, bold goals of their own.

WHAT DO YOU THINK?

Do you think that people should try to set records when it is a costly exercise and may put their lives and the lives of others at risk?

PRO

I think it is great that people want to go faster, higher, and be better. That sort of determination leads people to invent new things and improve our world.

Every adventurer realizes that his or her goals involve costs. Sometimes the cost might be the most priceless thing of all – life itself.

A wise adventurer takes many steps to be safe, but sometimes things go wrong. Sometimes people need to come to the rescue.

CON

I don't think people should waste time, money, and natural resources just to go faster or higher. There are more important things we can do to make a difference in the world.

GLOSSARY

Catamaran

ascent (*uh SENT*) upward movement

catamaran (*kat uh muh RAN*)
a boat with two hulls, or main frame
parts, that are joined together

challenge something that makes
you work harder and achieve more

continent (*KON tuh nuhnt*)
one of the seven land masses that make up the earth

descend (*di SEND*) to go down to a lower level

determination (*di tur min AY shun*) to have made a firm decision
to do something

equator an imaginary line around the middle of the earth, halfway
between the North and South poles

parachute (*PAR uh shoot*) a device made up of a fabric canopy with
a harness, which allows someone to float gently down to the ground

perseverance (*pur suh VEER ince*) determination to keep on trying
without giving up, even in difficult times

rupture (*RUHP chur*) to burst

solo alone

summit the highest point; at the top

temperamental moody and unpredictable

FIND OUT MORE

BOOKS

Bach, Julie S. *Sailing*. Smart Apple Media, 2000.

Bledsoe, Glen and Karen E. *Ballooning Adventures*. Capstone Books, 2000.

Chester, Jonathan. *The Young Adventurer's Guide to Everest: From Avalanche to Zopkio*. Tricycle Press, 2005.

Iwinski, Melissa. *The Wind at Work*. Scholastic Inc., 2008.

Nahum, Andrew. *Flying Machine*. DK Eyewitness Books, 2004.

Rinard, Judith E. *The Story of Flight: Smithsonian National Air and Space Museum*. Firefly Books, 2002.

WEB SITES

Go to the Web sites below to learn more about Steve Fossett and adventure sports.

www.stevefossett.com

www.iditarod.com/learn

www.myhero.com (search for "Steve Fossett")

http://solospirit.wustl.edu

INDEX

ABOUT THE AUTHOR

Laura Layton Strom is the author of many fiction and nonfiction books for children. She has worked as an educational writer, editor, and publisher for more than 20 years. Laura interviewed Steve Fossett for this book while he was in Argentina, trying for new glider records. She greatly admires Fossett's can-do attitude and hopes kids are inspired to reach for their dreams as well.